The Stu
Confirmation Version

Witherspoon Press
Louisville, Kentucky

Book design by Carol Eberhart Johnson

Published by Witherspoon Press, a Ministry of the General Assembly Council, Congregational Ministries Publishing, Presbyterian Church (U.S.A.), Louisville, Kentucky

Printed in the United States of America

08 09 10 11 12 — 10 9 8 7 6 5

Library of Congress Cataloging-in-Publication Data

The study catechism : confirmation version.
   p.cm.
 ISBN 978-1-57153-037-0
 1. Presbyterian Church—Catechisms—English.2,
Confirmation—Presbyterian Church. 1. Witherspoon Press.
 BX9184.S78.2002
 238'.5137—dc21
                2002154099

Introduction

Catechisms may seem hopelessly out of date, suggesting rote memorization of abstract answers to questions no one is asking. We live in the Internet age, not the era of McGuffey's Readers! We belong to a church of open inquiry, not one of pat answers! Catechisms may seem to be relics of an educational era that, thankfully, is in the past. Why, then, did the Presbyterian Church (U.S.A.) approve three new catechisms in 1998, and why are they being published for use in Presbyterian congregations and homes?

Catechisms have been part of Reformed church life since the sixteenth-century Reformation. Three catechisms are included in the *Book of Confessions*—the Heidelberg Catechism, and the Westminster Larger and Shorter Catechisms. They were not meant to be memorized (that was a nineteenth-century "innovation"), but rather to be used as brief summaries of Christian faith and life, presented in dialogue form. Reformed catechisms have helped generations of Christians to explore the Apostles' Creed, the Ten Commandments, and the Lord's Prayer by posing honest questions and providing faithful and relevant answers.

The Heidelberg Catechism's teaching on the Ten Commandments is as suggestive today as it was 450 years ago. A good example is the series of questions and answers on the sixth commandment, "You shall not kill."

Q: What does God require in the sixth commandment?

A: That I am not to abuse, hate, injure, or kill my neighbor, either with thought, or by word or gesture, much less by deed, whether by myself or through another, but to lay aside all desire for revenge; and that I do not harm myself or willingly expose myself to danger. This is why the authorities are armed with the means to prevent murder.

Introduction

Q: But does this commandment speak only of killing?

A: In forbidding murder God means to teach us that he abhors the root of murder, which is envy, hatred, anger, and desire for revenge, and that he regards all these as hidden murder.

Q: Is it enough, then, if we do not kill our neighbor in any of these ways?

A: No; for when God condemns envy, hatred, and anger, he requires us to love our neighbor as ourselves, to show patience, peace, gentleness, mercy, and friendliness toward him, to prevent injury to him as much as we can, also to do good to our enemies.

Notice how the catechism gives depth to the commandment, drawing upon the richness of Old Testament wisdom about the Law and New Testament teaching about love for neighbors. Notice, too, how the questions and answers move toward a positive appropriation of the commandment, pointing us beyond prohibitions and toward discipleship. Heidelberg's answers raise other questions, of course. And that is precisely the point! Catechisms are not intended to be the final word but the opening exchanges in a dialogue of faith that carries the conversation broader and deeper.

Catechisms can be a valuable part of catechesis—the ongoing process of instruction that is central to the formation of faith and faithfulness in the lives of believers. Faith formation, even in formal educational settings, is a rich process that employs a wide variety of methods and resources. Catechisms are not the only educational means at the church's disposal, but they are a valuable way of initiating a two-way conversation about Christian faith and life.

The new catechisms of the Presbyterian Church (U.S.A.) are designed for persons of different ages.

Belonging to God: A First Catechism is intended for children, beginning in the third or fourth grade. It departs from the traditional catechism format (Creed, Commandments, Lord's Prayer) and follows the general contours of the biblical narrative. Scripture verses are correlated with each question and answer. Belonging to God helps children understand the Bible in its relationship to God's love and our lives.

The Study Catechism: Full Version is intended for adults and older adolescents. It is suitable for study by new members of the church, college groups, adults in study groups, and church officers, in a variety of settings. Following the traditional format, the catechism strives to balance theological depth and accessibility.

The Study Catechism: Confirmation Version is a somewhat briefer and simpler version of The Study Catechism, suitable for use with confirmation classes composed of early adolescents.

These new catechisms are not "updates" of the church's earlier catechisms, but they do respond to contemporary concerns. The Study Catechism includes explorations of religious pluralism, science and faith, the shape of mission, and other pertinent issues, all in the context of basic Christian affirmations. The intention throughout is to acknowledge real questions and provide honest Christian answers in a way that encourages continued exploration.

The new Presbyterian Catechisms, used in whole or in part, can be an engaging means to enrich the educational ministry of the church, drawing children, youth, and adults into conversation with the whole church about believing and living as Christ's people in a world that hungers for the good news.

Joseph D. Small
Associate Director
Theology Worship and Discipleship
Presbyterian Church (U.S.A.)

The Study Catechism:
Confirmation Version

Question 1. What is God's purpose for your life?

God wills that I should live by the grace of the Lord Jesus Christ, for the love of God, and in the communion of the Holy Spirit.

> *2 Cor. 13:13* The grace of the Lord Jesus Christ, the love of God, and the communion of the Holy Spirit be with all of you.

Question 2. How do you live by the grace of the Lord Jesus Christ?

I am not my own. I have been bought with a price. The Lord Jesus Christ loved me and gave himself for me. I entrust myself completely to his care, giving thanks each day for his wonderful goodness.

> *1 Cor. 6:19–20* Or do you not know that your body is a temple of the Holy Spirit within you, which you have from God, and that you are not your own? For you were bought with a price; therefore glorify God in your body.

> *Gal. 2:20* It is no longer I who live, but it is Christ who lives in me. And the life I now live in the flesh I live by faith in the Son of God, who loved me and gave his life for me.

> *Ps. 136:1* O give thanks to the LORD, for he is good, for his steadfast love endures forever.

Question 3. How do you live for the love of God?

I love because God first loved me. Amazed by grace, I live for the Lord who died and rose again, triumphant over death, for my sake. Therefore, I take those around me to heart, especially those in need, knowing that Christ died for them no less than for me.

1 John 4:19 We love because he first loved us.

2 Cor. 5:15 And he died for all, so that those who live might live no longer for themselves, but for him who died and was raised for them.

Rom. 12:15–16 Rejoice with those who rejoice, weep with those who weep. Live in harmony with one another; do not be haughty, but associate with the lowly; do not claim to be wiser than you are.

Question 4. How do you live in the communion of the Holy Spirit?

By the Holy Spirit, I am made one with the Lord Jesus Christ. I am baptized into Christ's body, the church. As a member of this community, I trust in God's Word, share in the Lord's Supper, and turn to God in prayer. As I grow in grace and knowledge, I am led to do the good works that God intends for my life.

1 Cor. 12:27 Now you are the body of Christ and individually members of it.

Gal. 3:27 As many of you as were baptized into Christ have clothed yourselves with Christ.

1 Cor. 6:17, 19 But anyone united to the Lord becomes one spirit with him. . . . Or do you not know that your body is a temple of the Holy Spirit within you, which you have from God, and that you are not your own?

2 Peter 3:18 But grow in the grace and knowledge of our Lord and Savior Jesus Christ. To him be the glory both now and to the day of eternity. Amen.

Eph. 2:10 For we are what he has made us, created in Christ Jesus for good works, which God prepared beforehand to be our way of life.

I. The Apostles' Creed

Question 5. What does a Christian believe?

All that is promised in the gospel. A summary is found in the Apostles' Creed, which affirms the main content of the Christian faith.

> *John 20:31* But these are written so that you may come to believe that Jesus is the Messiah, the Son of God, and that through believing you may have life in his name.

Question 6. What is the first article of the Apostles' Creed?

"I believe in God the Father Almighty, Maker of heaven and earth."

Question 7. What do you believe when you confess your faith in "God the Father Almighty"?

That God is a God of love, and that God's love is powerful beyond measure.

> *Lam. 3:22* The steadfast love of the LORD never ceases, his mercies never come to an end.

> *Song 8:7* Many waters cannot quench love, neither can floods drown it. If one offered for love all the wealth of his house, it would be utterly scorned.

> *1 John 4:8* Whoever does not love does not know God, for God is love.

Question 8. How do you understand the love and power of God?

Through Jesus Christ. In his life of compassion, his death on the cross, and his resurrection from the dead, I see how vast is God's love for the world—a love that is ready to suffer for our sakes, yet so strong that nothing will prevail against it.

John 3:16 For God so loved the world that he gave his only Son, so that everyone who believes in him may not perish but may have eternal life.

Heb. 1:3 He is the reflection of God's glory and the exact imprint of God's very being, and he sustains all things by his powerful word.

1 John 4:9 God's love was revealed among us in this way: God sent his only Son into the world so that we might live through him.

Matt. 9:36 When he saw the crowds, he had compassion for them, because they were harassed and helpless, like sheep without a shepherd.

Ps. 106:8 Yet he saved them for his name's sake, so that he might make known his mighty power.

Question 9. What comfort do you receive from this truth?

This powerful and loving God is the one whose promises I may trust in all the circumstances of my life, and to whom I belong in life and in death.

Ps. 12:6 The promises of the LORD are promises that are pure, silver refined in a furnace on the ground, purified seven times.

Rom. 8:38–39 For I am convinced that neither death, nor life, nor angels, nor rulers, nor things present, nor things to come, nor powers, nor height, nor depth, nor anything else in all creation, will be able to separate us from the love of God in Jesus Christ our Lord.

Question 10. Do you make this confession by yourself?

No. With all those before me who have loved the Lord Jesus Christ, and with all who serve him on earth here and now, I confess my faith in this loving and powerful God.

Heb. 12:1 Therefore, since we are surrounded by so great a cloud of witnesses, let us also lay aside every weight and the sin that clings so closely, and let us run with perseverance the race that is set before us. . . .

Rom. 1:12 [I am longing to see you] so that we may be mutually encouraged by each other's faith, both yours and mine.

Question 11. When the creed speaks of "God the Father," does it mean that God is male?

No. Only creatures having bodies can be either male or female. But God has no body, since by nature God is Spirit. Holy Scripture reveals God as a living God beyond all sexual distinctions. Scripture uses diverse images for God, female as well as male.

Isa. 49:15 Can a woman forget her nursing child, or show no compassion for the child of her womb? Even these may forget, yet I will not forget you.

Isa. 66:13 As a mother comforts her child, so I will comfort you; you shall be comforted in Jerusalem.

Matt. 23:37 Jerusalem, Jerusalem, the city that kills the prophets and stones those who are sent to it! How often have I desired to gather your children together as a hen gathers her brood under her wings, and you were not willing!

Question 12. Why then does the creed speak of God the Father?

Because God is identified in the New Testament as the Father of our Lord Jesus Christ.

Rom. 1:7 To all God's beloved in Rome, who are called to be saints: Grace to you and peace from God our Father and the Lord Jesus Christ.

John 14:9–10 Jesus said to them, "Have I been with you all this time, Philip, and you still do not know me? Whoever has seen me has seen the Father. How can you say, 'Show us the Father'? Do you not believe that I am in the Father and the Father is in me? The words that I say to you I do not speak on my own; but the Father who dwells in me does his works."

John 17:24 Father, I desire that those also, whom you have given me, may be with me where I am, to see my glory, which you have given me because you loved me before the foundation of the world.

John 1:12 But to all who received him, who believed in his name, he gave power to become children of God. . . .

Gal. 4:6 And because you are children, God has sent the Spirit of his Son into our hearts, crying, "Abba! Father!"

Question 13. When you confess God as our Father, do you mean that men should dominate women?

No. All human beings, male or female, ought to conform their lives to the love, humility, and kindness of God. In fact God calls women and men to all ministries of the church. Any abuse or domination in human relationships is a direct violation of God's Fatherhood.

Gal. 3:28 There is no longer Jew or Greek, there is no longer slave or free, there is no longer male or female; for all of you are one in Christ Jesus.

Eph. 5:21 Be subject to one another out of reverence for Christ.

Question 14. If God's love is so powerful, why is there evil in the world?

No one can say why, for evil is a terrible mystery. Still, we know that God's triumph over evil is certain. Our Lord

Jesus Christ, crucified and risen, is himself God's promise that suffering will come to an end, that death shall be no more, and that all things will be made new.

Ps. 23:4 Even though I walk through the darkest valley, I fear no evil; for you are with me; your rod and your staff—they comfort me.

1 Peter 1:3 Blessed be the God and Father of our Lord Jesus Christ! By his great mercy he has given us a new birth into a living hope through the resurrection of Jesus Christ from the dead.

2 Peter 3:13 But, in accordance with his promise, we wait for new heavens and a new earth, where righteousness is at home.

Rom. 8:21 The creation itself will be set free from its bondage to decay and will obtain the freedom of the glory of the children of God.

Job 19:25 For I know that my Redeemer lives, and that at the last he will stand upon the earth.

Question 15. What do you believe when you say that God is "Maker of heaven and earth"?

First, that God called heaven and earth, with all that is in them, into being out of nothing. Second, that God rules and supports the creation in perfect wisdom, according to God's eternal purpose.

Rev. 4:11 You are worthy, our Lord and God, to receive glory and honor and power, for you created all things, and by your will they existed and were created.

Gen. 1:1 In the beginning when God created the heavens and the earth, the earth was a formless void and darkness covered the face of the deep, while a wind from God swept over the face of the waters.

Heb. 11:3 By faith we understand that the worlds were

prepared by the word of God, so that what is seen was made from things that are not visible.

Question 16. Did God need to make the world?

No. God would still be God even if heaven and earth had never been made.

> *Acts 17:24–25* The God who made the world and everything in it, he who is Lord of heaven and earth, does not live in shrines made by human hands, nor is he served by human hands, as though he needed anything, since he himself gives to all mortals life and breath and all things.

Question 17. Why, then, did God create the world?

God's creation of the world was an act of grace. God granted existence to the world simply in order to bless it. God created the world to reveal God's glory, to share the love and freedom at the heart of God's being, and to give us eternal life in fellowship with God.

> *Ps. 19:1* The heavens are telling the glory of God; and the firmament proclaims his handiwork.

> *2 Cor. 3:17* Now the Lord is the Spirit, and where the Spirit of the Lord is, there is freedom.

> *Ps. 67:6–7* The earth has yielded its increase; God, our God, has blessed us. May God continue to bless us; let all the ends of the earth revere him.

> *Eph. 1:3–4* Blessed be the God and Father of our Lord Jesus Christ, who has blessed us in Christ with every spiritual blessing in the heavenly places, just as he chose us in Christ before the foundation of the world to be holy and blameless before him in love.

> *John 3:36* Whoever believes in the Son has eternal life; whoever disobeys the Son will not see life, but must endure God's wrath.

Question 18. Does your confession of God as Creator contradict the findings of modern science?

No. Natural science has much to teach us about the particular mechanisms of nature, but it is not equipped to answer questions about ultimate reality. Nothing basic to the Christian faith contradicts the findings of modern science, nor does anything essential to modern science contradict the Christian faith.

> *John 1:1–3* In the beginning was the Word, and the Word was with God, and the Word was God. He was in the beginning with God. All things came into being through him, and without him not one thing came into being.

Question 19. What does it mean to say that human beings are created in the image of God?

God created us to live together in love and freedom—with God, with one another, and with the world. We are created to be loving companions of others so that something of God's goodness may be reflected in our lives.

> *Gen. 1:26* Then God said, "Let us make humankind in our image, according to our likeness: and let them have dominion over the fish of the sea, and over the birds of the air, and over the cattle, and over all the wild animals of the earth, and over every creeping thing that creeps upon the earth."

> *Gen. 1:27* So God created humankind in his image, in the image of God he created them; male and female he created them.

Question 20. What does our creation in God's image reflect about God?

Our being created for loving relationships is a reflection of the Holy Trinity. In the mystery of the one God, the three divine persons—Father, Son, and Holy Spirit—live eternally in perfect love and freedom.

Luke 3:21–22 Now when all the people were baptized, and when Jesus also had been baptized and was praying, the heaven was opened, and the Holy Spirit descended upon him in bodily form like a dove. And a voice came from heaven, "You are my Son, my Beloved; with you I am well pleased."

John 1:18 No one has ever seen God. It is God the only Son, who is close to the Father's heart, who has made him known.

John 5:19 Jesus said to them, "Very truly, I tell you, the Son can do nothing on his own, but only what he sees the Father doing; for whatever the Father does, the Son does likewise."

John 17:21–22 As you, Father, are in me and I am in you, may they also be in us, so that the world may believe that you have sent me. The glory that you have given me I have given them, so that they may be one, as we are one. . . .

Question 21. What does our creation in God's image say about our responsibility for the earth?

We are responsible for seeing that the earth's gifts are used fairly and wisely. We must take care that no creature suffers from the abuse of what we are given, and that future generations may continue to enjoy the earth's abundance in praise to God.

Ps. 24:1 The earth is the LORD's and all that is in it, the world, and those who live in it. . . .

Ps. 89:11 The heavens are yours, the earth also is yours; the world and all that is in it—you have founded them.

Gen. 2:15 The LORD God took the man and put him in the garden of Eden to till it and keep it.

Gen. 1:26 Then God said, "Let us make humankind in our image, according to our likeness; and let them have dominion over the fish of the sea, and over the birds of the air, and over the cattle, and over all the wild animals of the earth, and over every creeping thing that creeps upon the earth."

Isa. 24:5 The earth lies polluted under its inhabitants; for they have transgressed laws, violated the statutes, broken the everlasting covenant.

Rom. 12:2 Do not be conformed to this world, but be transformed by the renewing of your minds, so that you may discern what is the will of God—what is good and acceptable and perfect.

Question 22. What is God's providence?

God not only preserves the world, but also continually rules over it. God cares for every creature and brings good out of evil, so that nothing evil is permitted to occur that God does not bend finally to the good.

Rom. 8:28 We know that all things work together for good for those who love God, who are called according to his purpose.

Ps. 103:19 The LORD has established his throne in the heavens, and his kingdom rules over all.

Ps. 145:17 The LORD is just in all his ways, and kind in all his doings.

Question 23. What comfort do you receive by trusting in God's providence?

The eternal Father of our Lord Jesus Christ watches over me each day of my life, blessing and guiding me wherever I may be. God strengthens me when I am faithful, comforts me when I am discouraged or sorrowful, raises me up if I fall, and brings me at last to eternal life.

Ps. 146:9 The LORD watches over the strangers; he upholds the orphan and the widow, but the way of the wicked he brings to ruin.

Isa. 58:11 The LORD will guide you continually, and satisfy your needs in parched places, and make your bones strong; and you shall be like a watered garden, like a spring of water, whose waters never fail.

Isa. 41:10 Do not fear, for I am with you, do not be afraid, for I am your God; I will strengthen you, I will help you, I will uphold you with my victorious right hand.

2 Cor. 1:3–5 Blessed be the God and Father of our Lord Jesus Christ, the Father of mercies and the God of all consolation, who consoles us in all our affliction, so that we may be able to console those who are in any affliction with the consolation with which we ourselves are consoled by God.

Ps. 30:5 For his anger is but for a moment; his favor is for a lifetime. Weeping may linger for the night, but joy comes in the morning.

Question 24. What is the second article of the Apostles' Creed?

"And I believe in Jesus Christ, his only Son, our Lord. He was conceived by the Holy Spirit, born of the Virgin Mary, suffered under Pontius Pilate, was crucified, dead and buried. He descended into hell. On the third day he rose again from the dead. He ascended into heaven and is seated at the right hand of the Father. He will come again to judge the living and the dead."

Question 25. What do you believe when you confess your faith in Jesus Christ as "God's only Son"?

No one else will ever be God incarnate. No one else will ever die for the sins of the world. Only Jesus Christ is such a person, only he could do such a work, and he in fact has done it.

Isa. 53:5 But he was wounded for our transgressions, crushed for our iniquities; upon him was the punishment that made us whole, and by his bruises we are healed.

John 1:29 The next day he saw Jesus coming toward him and declared, "Here is the Lamb of God who takes away the sin of the world!"

Col. 1:15–20 He is the image of the invisible God, the firstborn of all creation; for in him all things in heaven and on earth were created, things visible and invisible, whether thrones or dominions or rulers or powers—all things have been created through him and for him. He himself is before all things, and in him all things hold together. He is the head of the body, the church; he is the beginning, the firstborn from the dead, so that he might come to have first place in everything. For in him all the fullness of God was pleased to dwell, and through him God was pleased to reconcile to himself all things, whether on earth or in heaven, by making peace through the blood of his cross.

Luke 3:21–22 Now when all the people were baptized, and when Jesus also had been baptized and was praying, the heaven was opened, and the Holy Spirit descended upon him in bodily form like a dove. And a voice came from heaven, "You are my Son, the Beloved; with you I am well pleased."

John 1:14 And the Word became flesh and lived among us, and we have seen his glory, the glory as of a father's only son, full of grace and truth.

Question 26. What do you affirm when you confess your faith in Jesus Christ as "our Lord"?

That having been raised from the dead Christ reigns with compassion and justice over all things in heaven and on earth, especially over those who confess him by faith. By loving and serving him above all else, I give glory and honor to God.

1 Cor. 15:3–4 For I handed on to you as of first importance what I in turn had received: that Christ died for our sins in accordance with the scriptures, and that he was buried, and that he was raised on the third day in accordance with the scriptures. . . .

Rev. 11:15 Then the seventh angel blew his trumpet, and there were loud voices in heaven, saying, "The kingdom of the world has become the kingdom of our Lord and of his Messiah, and he will reign forever and ever."

Eph. 1:20–23 God put this power to work in Christ when he raised him from the dead and seated him at his right hand in the heavenly places, far above all rule and authority and power and dominion, and above every name that is named, not only in this age but also in the age to come. And he has put all things under his feet and has made him the head over all things for the church, which is his body, the fullness of him who fills all in all.

Phil. 2:9–11 Therefore God also highly exalted him and gave him the name that is above every name, so that at the name of Jesus every knee should bend, in heaven and on earth and under the earth, and every tongue should confess that Jesus Christ is Lord, to the glory of God the Father.

Question 27. How did the coming of Jesus confirm God's covenant with Israel?

God made a covenant with Israel, promising that God would be their God, that they would be God's people, and that through them all the peoples of the earth would be blessed. With the coming of Jesus the covenant was thrown open to the world. By faith in him, all peoples were welcomed into the covenant. This throwing open of the gates confirmed the promise that through Israel God's blessing would come to all.

Gen. 17:3–4 Then Abram fell on his face; and God said to him, "As for me, this is my covenant with you: You shall be the ancestor of a multitude of nations."

Gen. 12:1–3 Now the LORD said to Abram, "Go from your country and your kindred and your father's house to the land that I will show you. I will make of you a great nation, and I will bless you, and make your name great, so that you will be a blessing. I will bless those who bless you, and the one who curses you I will curse; and in you all the families of the earth shall be blessed."

Ex. 6:4–5 I also established my covenant with them, to give them the land of Canaan, the land in which they resided as aliens. I have also heard the groaning of the Israelites whom the Egyptians are holding as slaves, and I have remembered my covenant.

Gal. 3:14 . . . in order that in Christ Jesus the blessing of Abraham might come to the Gentiles, so that we might receive the promise of the Spirit through faith.

Jer. 30:22 And you shall be my people, and I will be your God.

1 Peter 2:9–10 But you are a chosen race, a royal priesthood, a holy nation, God's own people, in order that you might proclaim the mighty acts of him who called you out of darkness into his marvelous light. Once you were not a people, but now you are God's people; once you had not received mercy, but now you have received mercy.

Zech. 1:6 But my words and my statutes, which I commanded to my servants the prophets, did they not overtake your ancestors? So they repented and said, "The LORD of hosts has dealt with us according to our ways and deeds, just as he planned to do."

Lev. 5:6 And you shall bring to the LORD, as your penalty for the sin that you have committed, . . . a sheep or a goat, as a sin offering; and the priest shall make atonement on your behalf for your sin.

Ps. 72:1, 4 Give the king your justice, O God, and your righteousness to a king's son. . . . May he defend the cause of the poor of the people, give deliverance to the needy, and crush the oppressor.

Question 28. Was the covenant with Israel an everlasting covenant?

Yes. Although for the most part Israel has not accepted Jesus as the Messiah, God has not rejected Israel. God still loves Israel, and God is their hope, "for the gifts and the calling of God are irrevocable" (Rom. 11:29).

Isa. 61:8 For I the LORD love justice, I hate robbery and wrongdoing; I will faithfully give them their recompense, and I will make an everlasting covenant with them.

Jer. 31:3 I have loved you with an everlasting love; therefore, I have continued my faithfulness to you.

2 Sam. 23:5 Is not my house like this with God? For he has made with me an everlasting covenant, ordered in all things and secure. Will he not cause to prosper all my help and my desire?

Rom. 11:29 For the gifts and the calling of God are irrevocable.

Question 29. What do you affirm when you say he was "conceived by the Holy Spirit and born of the Virgin Mary"?

First, that being born of Mary, Jesus was truly a human being. Second, that our Lord's incarnation was a holy and mysterious event. Third, that he was set apart by his unique origin for the sake of accomplishing our salvation.

Luke 1:31 And now, you will conceive in your womb and bear a son, and you will name him Jesus.

Luke 1:35 The angel said to her, "The Holy Spirit will come upon you, and the power of the Most High will overshadow you; therefore the child to be born will be holy; he will be called Son of God."

Heb. 2:14 Since, therefore, the children share flesh and blood, he himself likewise shared the same things, so that through death he might destroy the one who has the power of death, that is, the devil. . . .

Phil. 2:5–7 Let the same mind be in you that was in Christ Jesus, who, though he was in the form of God, did not regard equality with God as something to be exploited, but emptied himself, taking the form of a slave, being born in human likeness.

Question 30. What is the significance of affirming that Jesus is truly God?

Only God can properly deserve worship. Only God can reveal to us who God is. And only God can save us from our sins. Being truly God, Jesus meets these conditions. He is the proper object of our worship, the self-revelation of God, and the Savior of the world.

John 20:28 Thomas answered him, "My Lord and my God!" Jesus said to him, "Have you believed because you have seen me? Blessed are those who have not seen and yet have come to believe."

Matt. 11:27 All things have been handed over to me by my Father; and no one knows the Son except the Father, and no one knows the Father except the Son and anyone to whom the Son chooses to reveal him.

1 John 4:14 And we have seen and do testify that the Father has sent his Son as the Savior of the world.

Question 31. What is the significance of affirming that Jesus is also truly a human being?

Being truly human, Jesus entered fully into our fallen situation and overcame it. He lived a life of pure obedience to God, even to the point of accepting a violent death. When we accept him by faith, he removes our disobedience and clothes us with his perfect righteousness.

> *Heb. 2:17–18* Therefore he had to become like his brothers and sisters in every respect, so that he might be a merciful and faithful high priest in the service of God, to make a sacrifice of atonement for the sins of the people. Because he himself was tested by what he suffered, he is able to help those who are being tested.

> *Heb. 4:15* For we do not have a high priest who is unable to sympathize with our weaknesses, but we have one who in every respect has been tested as we are, yet without sin.

> *Heb. 5:8–9* Although he was a Son, he learned obedience through what he suffered; and having been made perfect, he became the source of eternal salvation for all who obey him. . . .

> *Rom. 5:19* For just as by the one man's disobedience the many were made sinners, so by the one man's obedience the many will be made righteous.

Question 32. What do you affirm when you say that he "suffered under Pontius Pilate"?

First, that our Lord was rejected and abused by the authorities of that time, both religious and political. Second, and even more importantly, that he submitted to condemnation by an earthly judge so that we might be acquitted before our heavenly Judge.

> *Luke 18:32* For he will be handed over to the Gentiles; and he will be mocked and insulted and spat upon.

Isa. 53:3 He was despised and rejected by others; a man of suffering and acquainted with infirmity; and as one from whom others hide their faces he was despised, and we held him of no account.

Ps. 9:9 The LORD is a stronghold for the oppressed, a stronghold in times of trouble.

Luke 1:52 He has brought down the powerful from their thrones, and lifted up the lowly. . . .

2 Cor. 5:21 For our sake he made him to be sin who knew no sin, so that in him we might become the righteousness of God.

2 Tim. 4:8 From now on there is reserved for me a crown of righteousness, which the Lord, the righteous judge, will give me on that day, and not only to me but also to all who have longed for his appearing.

Question 33. What do you affirm when you say that he was "crucified, dead, and buried"?

From Christ's lonely and terrible death we learn that there is no sorrow he has not known, no grief he has not borne, and no price he was unwilling to pay in order to reconcile us to God.

Matt. 26:38–39 Then he said to them, "I am deeply grieved, even to death; remain here, and stay awake with me." And going a little farther, he threw himself on the ground and prayed, "My Father, if it is possible, let this cup pass from me; yet not what I want but what you want."

Isa. 53:5 But he was wounded for our transgressions, crushed for our iniquities; upon him was the punishment that made us whole, and by his bruises we are healed.

Gal. 3:13 Christ redeemed us from the curse of the law by becoming a curse for us—for it is written, "Cursed is everyone who hangs on a tree. . . ."

Heb. 2:9 But we do see Jesus, who for a little while was made lower than the angels, now crowned with glory and honor because of the suffering of death, so that by the grace of God he might taste death for everyone.

2 Cor. 5:19 In Christ God was reconciling the world to himself, not counting their trespasses against them, and entrusting the message of reconciliation to us.

Question 34. What do you affirm when you say that he "descended into hell"?

That our Lord took upon himself the full consequences of our sinfulness in order that we might be spared.

Mark 15:34 At three o'clock Jesus cried out with a loud voice, "Eloi, Eloi, lema sabachthani?" which means, "My God, my God, why have you forsaken me?"

Heb. 9:26 . . . for then he would have had to suffer again and again since the foundation of the world. But as it is, he has appeared once for all at the end of the age to remove sin by the sacrifice of himself.

Rom. 4:24–25 It will be reckoned to us who believe in him who raised Jesus our Lord from the dead, who was handed over to death for our trespasses and was raised for our justification.

Question 35. What do you affirm when you say that "on the third day he rose again from the dead"?

Our Lord could not be held by the power of death. Having died on the cross, he appeared to his followers, and revealed himself to them as the Lord and Savior of the world.

Acts 2:24 But God raised him up, having freed him from death, because it was impossible for him to be held in its power.

1 Cor. 15:3–4 For I handed on to you as of first importance what I in turn had received: that Christ died for our sins in accordance with the scriptures, and that he was buried, and that he was raised on the third day in accordance with the scriptures. . . .

Luke 24:36–40 While they were talking about this, Jesus himself stood among them and said to them, "Peace be with you." They were startled and terrified, and thought that they were seeing a ghost. He said to them, "Why are you frightened, and why do doubts arise in your hearts? Look at my hands and my feet; see that it is I myself. Touch me and see; for a ghost does not have flesh and bones as you see that I have." And when he had said this, he showed them his hands and his feet.

John 20:15–18 Jesus said to her, "Woman, why are you weeping? Whom are you looking for?" Supposing him to be the gardener, she said to him, "Sir, if you have carried him away, tell me where you have laid him, and I will take him away," Jesus said to her, "Mary!" She turned and said to him in Hebrew, "Rabbouni!" (which means teacher). Jesus said to her, "Do not hold on to me, because I have not yet ascended to the Father. But go to my brothers and say to them, 'I am ascending to my Father and your Father, to my God and your God.'" Mary Magdalene went and announced to the disciples, "I have seen the Lord"; and she told them that he had said these things to her.

1 Cor. 15:5–8 . . . and that he appeared to Cephas, then to the twelve. Then he appeared to more than five hundred brothers and sisters at one time, most of whom are still alive, though some have died. Then he appeared to James, then to all the apostles. Last of all, as to one untimely born, he appeared also to me.

John 20:27 Then he said to Thomas, "Put your finger here and see my hands. Reach out your hand and put it in my side. Do not doubt but believe."

Question 36. What do you affirm when you say that "he ascended into heaven and is seated at the right hand of the Father"?

First, that Christ has gone to be with his loving Father so that he is now hidden except to the eyes of faith. Second, however, that he is not cut off from us but is present here and now by grace. He reigns with divine authority, protecting us, guiding us, and interceding for us until he returns in glory.

> *Acts 1:6–11* So when they had come together, they asked him, "Lord, is this the time when you will restore the kingdom to Israel?" He replied, "It is not for you to know the times or periods that the Father has set by his own authority. But you will receive power when the Holy Spirit has come upon you; and you will be my witnesses in Jerusalem, in all Judea and Samaria, and to the ends of the earth." When he had said this, as they were watching, he was lifted up, and a cloud took him out of their sight. While he was going and they were gazing up toward heaven, suddenly two men in white robes stood by them. They said, "Men of Galilee, why do you stand looking up toward heaven? This Jesus, who has been taken up from you into heaven, will come in the same way as you saw him go into heaven."

> *Col. 3:1* So if you have been raised with Christ, seek the things that are above, where Christ is, seated at the right hand of God.

Question 37. How do you understand the words that "he will come again to judge the living and the dead"?

Like everyone else, I too must stand in fear and trembling before the judgment seat of Christ. But the Judge is the one who submitted to judgment for my sake. Nothing will be able to separate me from the love of God in Christ Jesus my Lord.

2 Cor. 5:10 For all of us must appear before the judgment seat of Christ, so that each may receive recompense for what has been done in the body, whether good or evil.

Eccl. 12:14 For God will bring every deed into judgment, including every secret thing, whether good or evil.

Acts 17:31 . . . because he has fixed a day on which he will have the world judged in righteousness by a man whom he has appointed, and of this he has given assurance to all by raising him from the dead.

Rom. 8:38–39 For I am convinced that neither death, nor life, nor angels, nor rulers, nor things present, nor things to come, nor powers, nor height, nor depth, nor anything else in all creation, will be able to separate us from the love of God in Christ Jesus our Lord.

1 John 4:17 Love has been perfected among us in this: that we may have boldness on the day of judgment, because as he is, so are we in this world.

1 Cor. 3:12–15 Now if anyone builds on the foundation with gold, silver, precious stones, wood, hay, straw— the work of each builder will become visible, for the Day will disclose it, because it will be revealed with fire, and the fire will test what sort of work each has done. If what has been built on the foundation survives, the builder will receive a reward. If the work is burned up, the builder will suffer loss; the builder will be saved, but only as through fire.

Acts 10:42 He commanded us to preach to the people and to testify that he is the one ordained by God as judge of the living and the dead.

Question 38. Will all human beings be saved?

No one will be lost who can be saved. The limits to salvation, whatever they may be, are known only to God. Three truths above all are certain. God is a holy God who is not to be trifled with. No one will be saved except by grace alone. And no judge could possibly be more gracious than our Lord and Savior, Jesus Christ.

Heb. 10:31 It is a fearful thing to fall into the hands of the living God.

Rom. 11:32 For God has imprisoned all in disobedience so that he may be merciful to all.

Luke 15:4–7 Which one of you, having a hundred sheep and losing one of them, does not leave the ninety-nine in the wilderness and go after the one that is lost until he finds it? When he has found it, he lays it on his shoulders and rejoices. And when he comes home, he calls together his friends and neighbors, saying to them, "Rejoice with me, for I have found my sheep that was lost." Just so, I tell you, there will be more joy in heaven over one sinner who repents than over ninety-nine righteous persons who need no repentance.

Eph. 2:8 For by grace you have been saved through faith, and this is not your own doing; it is the gift of God. . . .

1 Tim. 2:3–4 This is right and is acceptable in the sight of God our Savior, who desires everyone to be saved and to come to the knowledge of the truth.

John 3:17–18 Indeed, God did not send the Son into the world to condemn the world, but in order that the world might be saved through him. Those who believe in him are not condemned; but those who do not yet believe are condemned already, because they have not believed in the name of the only Son of God.

Ezek. 18:32 For I have no pleasure in the death of anyone, says the Lord GOD. Turn, then, and live.

2 Cor. 5:14–15 For the love of Christ urges us on, because we are convinced that one has died for all; therefore all have died. And he died for all, so that those who live might live no longer for themselves, but for him who died and was raised for them.

Question 39. How should I treat non-Christians and people of other religions?

I should meet friendship with friendship, hostility with kindness, generosity with gratitude, persecution with forbearance, truth with agreement, and error with truth. I should express my faith by word and by deed. I should avoid compromising the truth on the one hand and being narrow-minded on the other. In short, I should welcome and accept these others in a way that honors and reflects the Lord's welcome and acceptance of me.

Rom. 15:7 Welcome one another, therefore, just as Christ has welcomed you, for the glory of God.

Luke 6:37 Do not judge, and you will not be judged; do not condemn, and you will not be condemned. Forgive, and you will be forgiven.

Matt. 5:44 But I say to you, Love your enemies and pray for those who persecute you. . . .

Eph. 4:25 So then, putting away falsehood, let all of us speak the truth to our neighbors, for we are members of one another.

Acts 13:47 For so the Lord has commanded us, saying, "I have set you to be a light for the Gentiles, so that you may bring salvation to the ends of the earth."

Rom. 12:21 Do not be overcome by evil, but overcome evil with good.

Rom. 13:10 Love does no wrong to a neighbor; therefore, love is the fulfilling of the law.

Question 40. How will God deal with the followers of other religions?

God offers salvation to all human beings through Jesus Christ. How God will deal with those who do not know or follow Christ, but who follow another tradition, we cannot finally say. We can say, however, that God is gracious and merciful, and that God will not deal with people in any other way than we see in Jesus Christ, who came as the Savior of the world.

Rev. 7:9 After this I looked, and there was a great multitude that no one could count, from every nation, from all tribes and peoples and languages, standing before the throne and before the Lamb, robed in white, with palm branches in their hands.

Ps. 103:8 The LORD is merciful and gracious, slow to anger and abounding in steadfast love.

John 3:19 And this is the judgment, that the light of the world has come into the world, and people loved darkness rather than light because their deeds were evil.

Titus 2:11 For the grace of God has appeared, bringing salvation to all. . . .

Question 41. Is Christianity the only true religion?

By the grace of God, Christianity offers the truth of the gospel. Although other religions may contain various truths, no other can or does affirm the name of Jesus Christ as the hope of the world.

Matt. 7:3 Why do you see the speck in your neighbor's eye, but do not notice the log in your own eye?

James 1:26 If any think they are religious, and do not bridle their tongues but deceive their hearts, their religion is worthless.

James 1:27 Religion that is pure and undefiled before God, the Father, is this: to care for orphans and widows in their distress, and to keep oneself unstained by the world.

Acts 4:12 There is salvation in no one else, for there is no other name under heaven given among mortals by which we must be saved.

John 14:6 Jesus said to him, "I am the way, and the truth, and the life. No one comes to the Father except through me."

Rom. 1:16 For I am not ashamed of the gospel; it is the power of God for salvation for everyone who has faith, to the Jew first and also to the Greek.

2 Cor. 4:7 But we have this treasure in clay jars, so that it may be made clear that this extraordinary power belongs to God and does not come from us.

Question 42. What is the third article of the Apostles' Creed?

"I believe in the Holy Spirit, the holy catholic church, the communion of saints, the forgiveness of sins, the resurrection of the body, and the life everlasting. Amen."

Question 43. What do you believe when you confess your faith in the Holy Spirit?

The Holy Spirit is the divine person who enables us to love, know, and serve Jesus Christ.

John 14:26 But the Advocate, the Holy Spirit, whom the Father will send in my name, will teach you everything, and remind you of all that I have said to you.

1 Cor. 12:3 Therefore I want you to understand that no one speaking by the Spirit of God ever says "Let Jesus be cursed!" and no one can say "Jesus is Lord" except by the Holy Spirit.

Rom. 5:5 . . . and hope does not disappoint us, because God's love has been poured into our hearts through the Holy Spirit that has been given to us.

1 Cor. 6:17, 19 But anyone united to the Lord becomes one spirit with him. . . . Or do you not know that your body is a temple of the Holy Spirit within you, which you have from God, and that you are not your own?

1 Cor. 3:16 Do you not know that you are God's temple and that God's Spirit dwells in you?

John 4:24 God is spirit, and those who worship him must worship in spirit and truth.

Question 44. How do we receive the Holy Spirit?

By receiving the Word of God. The Spirit arrives with the Word, brings us to rebirth, and assures us of eternal life. The Spirit nurtures, corrects, and strengthens us with the truth of the Word.

Eph. 6:17 Take the helmet of salvation, and the sword of the Spirit, which is the word of God.

John 14:16–17 And I will ask the Father, and he will give you another Advocate, to be with you forever. This is the Spirit of truth, whom the world cannot receive, because it neither sees him nor knows him. You know him, because he abides with you, and he will be in you.

John 3:5–6 Jesus answered, "Very truly I tell you, no one can enter the kingdom of God without being born of water and Spirit. What is born of the flesh is flesh, and what is born of the Spirit is spirit."

Luke 11:13 If you then, who are evil, know how to give good gifts to your children, how much more will the heavenly Father give the Holy Spirit to those who ask him!

1 Thess. 1:5 . . . because our message of the gospel came to you not in word only, but also in power and in the Holy Spirit and with full conviction; just as you know what kind of persons we proved to be among you for your sake.

John 16:8 And when he comes, he will prove the world wrong about sin and righteousness and judgment. . . .

Rom. 8:15–16 For you did not receive a spirit of slavery to fall back into fear, but you received a spirit of adoption. When we cry, "Abba! Father!" it is that very Spirit bearing witness with our spirit that we are children of God. . . .

1 Peter 2:2 Like newborn infants, long for the pure, spiritual milk, so that by it you may grow into salvation. . . .

Question 45. What do you mean when you speak of "the Word of God"?

"Jesus Christ, as he is attested for us in Holy Scripture, is the one Word of God which we have to hear and which we have to trust and obey in life and in death" (Barmen Declaration, Article I).

John 1:1–5 In the beginning was the Word, and the Word was with God, and the Word was God. He was in the beginning with God. All things came into being through him, and without him not one thing came into being. What has come into being with him was life, and the life was the light of all people. The light shines in the darkness, and the darkness did not overcome it.

John 1:14 And the Word become flesh and lived among us, and we have seen his glory, the glory as of a father's only son, full of grace and truth.

Question 46. Isn't Holy Scripture also the Word of God?

Yes. Holy Scripture is also God's Word because of its focus, its function, and its founder. Its central focus is Jesus Christ, the living Word. Its basic function is to deepen our love, knowledge, and service of him as our Savior and Lord. And its dependable founder is the Holy Spirit, who spoke through the prophets and apostles, and who inspires us with eager desire for the truths that Scripture contains.

2 Tim. 3:16 All scripture is inspired by God and is useful for teaching, for reproof, for correction, and for training in righteousness. . . .

John 5:39 You search the scriptures because you think that in them you have eternal life; and it is they that testify on my behalf.

Question 47. Isn't preaching also the Word of God?

Yes. Preaching is God's Word when it is faithful to the witness of Holy Scripture. Faith comes by hearing God's Word in the form of faithful preaching and teaching.

Mark 16:15 And he said to them, "Go into all the world and proclaim the good news to the whole creation."

2 Cor. 4:5 For we do not proclaim ourselves; we proclaim Jesus Christ as Lord and ourselves as your slaves for Jesus' sake.

Rom. 1:15–16 . . . hence my eagerness to proclaim the gospel to you also who are in Rome. For I am not ashamed of the gospel; it is the power of God for salvation to everyone who has faith, to the Jew first and also to the Greek.

Rom. 10:17 So faith comes from what is heard, and what is heard comes through the word of Christ.

Question 48. What do you affirm when you speak of "the holy catholic church"?

The church is the community of all faithful people who have given their lives to Jesus Christ with thanksgiving. The church is holy because he is holy, and universal (or "catholic") in significance because he is universal in significance. Despite all its remaining imperfections here and now, the church is called to become ever more holy and catholic, for that is what it already is in Christ.

Gal. 2:20 It is no longer I who live, but it is Christ who lives in me. And the life I now live in the flesh I live by faith in the Son of God, who loved me and gave himself for me.

1 Cor. 1:2 To the church of God that is in Corinth, to those who are sanctified in Christ Jesus, called to be saints, together with all those who in every place call on the name of our Lord Jesus Christ, both their Lord and ours. . . .

Lev. 11:44 For I am the LORD your God; sanctify yourselves therefore, and be holy, for I am holy.

1 Peter 1:15–16 Instead, as he who called you is holy, be holy yourselves in all your conduct; for it is written, "You shall be holy, for I am holy."

Rev. 5:9 They sing a new song: "You are worthy to take the scroll and to open its seals, for you were slaughtered and by your blood you ransomed for God saints from every tribe and language and people and nation. . . . "

Question 49. What is the mission of the church?

The mission of the church is to bear witness to God's love for the world in Jesus Christ.

Acts 1:8 But you will receive power when the Holy Spirit has come upon you; and you will be my witnesses in Jerusalem, in all Judea and Samaria, and to the ends of the earth.

John 15:26–27 When the Advocate comes, whom I will send to you from the Father, the Spirit of truth who comes from the Father, he will testify on my behalf. You also are to testify because you have been with me from the beginning.

Eph. 3:8–10 Although I am the very least of all the saints, this grace was given to me to bring to the Gentiles the news of the boundless riches of Christ, and to make everyone see what is the plan of the mystery hidden for ages in God who created all things; so that through the church the wisdom of God in its rich variety might now be made known to the rulers and authorities in the heavenly places.

Question 50. What forms does this mission take?

The church's mission takes a wide variety of forms, including evangelism, work for social justice, and ministries of care. Yet the center is always the same: Jesus Christ. In every case the church extends mercy and forgiveness to the needy in a way that points finally to him.

Luke 10:37 He said, "The one who showed him mercy." Jesus said to him, "Go and do likewise."

Eph. 4:32 Be kind to one another, tenderhearted, forgiving one another, as God in Christ has forgiven you.

Deut. 15:11 Since there will never cease to be some in need on the earth, I therefore command you, "Open your hand to the poor and needy neighbor in your land."

Acts 4:34 There was not a needy person among them, for as many as owned lands or houses sold them and brought the proceeds of what was sold.

Question 51. Who are the needy?

The hungry need bread, the homeless need a roof, the oppressed need justice, and the lonely need fellowship. At the same time—on another and deeper level—the hopeless need hope, sinners need forgiveness, and the world needs the gospel. On this level no one is excluded, and all the needy are one. Our mission as the church is to bring hope to a desperate world by declaring God's undying love—as one beggar tells another where to find bread.

Ps. 10:12 Rise up, O LORD; O God, lift up your hand; do not forget the oppressed.

Matt. 25:37–40 Then the righteous will answer him, "Lord, when was it that we saw you hungry and gave you food, or thirsty and gave you something to drink? And when was it that we saw you a stranger and welcomed you, or naked and gave you clothing? And when was it that we saw you sick or in prison and visited you?" And the king will answer them, "Truly I tell you, just as you did it to one of the least of these who are members of my family, you did it to me."

Jer. 9:23 Thus says the LORD: "Do not let the wise boast in their wisdom, do not let the mighty boast in their might, do not let the wealthy boast in their wealth. . . . "

1 Cor. 9:16 If I proclaim the gospel, this gives me no ground for boasting, for an obligation is laid on me, and woe to me if I do not proclaim the gospel!

Eph. 6:19 Pray also for me, so that when I speak, a message may be given to me to make known with boldness the mystery of the gospel. . . .

Question 52. What do you affirm when you speak of "the communion of saints"?

All those who live in union with Christ, whether on earth or with God in heaven, are "saints." Our communion with Christ makes us members one of another. The ties that bind us in Christ are deeper than any other human relationship.

Eph. 2:19–20 So then you are no longer strangers and aliens, but you are citizens with the saints and also members of the household of God, built upon the foundation of the apostles and prophets, with Christ Jesus himself as the cornerstone.

Rom. 12:5 . . . so we, who are many, are one body in Christ, and individually we are members one of another.

Eph. 2:14 For he is our peace; in his flesh he has made both groups into one and has broken down the dividing wall, that is, the hostility between us.

1 Cor. 12:27 Now you are the body of Christ and individually members of it.

Gal. 3:28 There is no longer Jew or Greek, there is no longer slave or free, there is no longer male and female; for all of you are one in Christ Jesus.

Eph. 4:4 There is one body and one Spirit, just as you were called to the one hope of your calling. . . .

1 Cor. 12:4–7, 12–13 Now there are varieties of gifts, but the same Spirit; and there are varieties of services, but the same Lord; and there are varieties of activities, but it is the same God who activates all of them in everyone. To each is given the manifestation of the Spirit for the common good. . . . For just as the body is one and has many members, and all the members of the body, though many, are one body, so it is with Christ. For in the one Spirit we were all baptized into one body—Jews or Greeks, slaves or free—and we were all made to drink of one Spirit.

Question 53. How do you enter into communion with Christ and so with one another?

By the power of the Holy Spirit as it works through Word and Sacrament. The Scriptures acknowledge two sacraments as instituted by our Lord Jesus Christ—baptism and the Lord's Supper.

1 Cor. 10:17 Because there is one bread, we who are many are one body, for we all partake of the one bread.

1 Cor. 12:13 For in the one Spirit we were all baptized into one body—Jews or Greeks, slaves or free—and we were all made to drink of one Spirit.

Col. 3:16 Let the word of Christ dwell in you richly; teach and admonish one another in all wisdom; and with gratitude in your hearts sing psalms, hymns, and spiritual songs to God.

Question 54. What is a sacrament?

A sacrament is a special act of Christian worship, instituted by Christ, which uses a visible sign to proclaim the promise of the gospel for the forgiveness of sins and eternal life. In baptism the sign is that of water; in the Lord's Supper, that of bread and wine.

Mark 1:9–11 In those days Jesus came from Nazareth of Galilee and was baptized by John in the Jordan. And just as he was coming up out of the water, he saw the heavens torn apart and the Spirit descending like a dove on him. And a voice came from heaven, "You are my Son, the Beloved; with you I am well pleased."

Mark 14:22–25 While they were eating, he took a loaf of bread, and after blessing it he broke it, gave it to them, and said, "Take; this is my body." Then he took a cup, and after giving thanks he gave it to them, and all of them drank from it. He said to them, "This is my blood of the covenant, which is poured out for many. Truly I tell you, I will never again drink of the fruit of the vine until that day when I drink it new in the kingdom of God."

Question 55. What is baptism?

Baptism is the sign and seal through which we are joined to Christ.

Rom. 6:3–4 Do you not know that all of us who have been baptized into Christ Jesus were baptized into his death? Therefore we have been buried with him by baptism into death, so that, just as Christ was raised from the dead by the glory of the Father, so we too might walk in newness of life.

Gal. 3:27 As many of you as were baptized into Christ have clothed yourselves with Christ.

Rom. 4:11 He received the sign of circumcision as a seal of the righteousness that he had by faith while he was still uncircumcised. The purpose was to make him the ancestor of all who believe without being circumcised and who thus have righteousness reckoned to them. . . .

Question 56. What does it mean to be baptized?

My baptism means that I am joined to Jesus Christ forever. As I am baptized with water, he baptizes me with his Spirit, washing away all my sins and freeing me from their control. My baptism is a sign that one day I will rise with him in glory, and may walk with him even now in newness of life.

Col. 2:12 When you were buried with him in baptism, you were also raised with him through faith in the power of God, who raised him from the dead.

Mark 1:8 I have baptized you with water; but he will baptize you with the Holy Spirit.

1 Cor. 6:11 And this is what some of you used to be. But you were washed, you were sanctified, you were justified in the name of the Lord Jesus Christ and in the Spirit of our God.

Eph. 4:4–6 There is one body and one Spirit, just as you were called to the one hope of your calling, one Lord, one faith, one baptism, one God and Father of all, who is above all and through all and in all.

Question 57. Are infants also to be baptized?

Yes. Along with their believing parents, they are included in the great hope of the gospel and belong to the people of God. Forgiveness and faith are both promised to them through Christ's covenant with his people.

Gen. 17:7 I will establish my covenant between me and you, and your offspring after you throughout their generations, for an everlasting covenant, to be God to you and to your offspring after you.

Acts 2:38–39 Peter said to them, "Repent, and be baptized every one of you in the name of Jesus Christ so that your sins may be forgiven; and you will receive the gift of the Holy Spirit. For the promise is for you, for your children, and for all who are far away, everyone whom the Lord our God calls to him."

Acts 16:15 When she and her household were baptized, she urged us, saying, "If you have judged me to be faithful to the Lord, come and stay at my home." And she prevailed upon us.

Acts 16:33 At the same hour of the night he took them and washed their wounds; then he and his entire family were baptized without delay.

Acts 18:8 Crispus, the official of the synagogue, became a believer in the Lord, together with all his household; and many of the Corinthians who heard Paul became believers and were baptized.

Question 58. Why are you baptized in the name of the Father, and of the Son, and of the Holy Spirit?

Because of the command Jesus gave his disciples. After he was raised from the dead, he appeared to them and said, "Go therefore and make disciples of all nations, baptizing them in the name of the Father and of the Son and of the Holy Spirit" (Matt. 28:19).

Matt. 28:16–20 Now the eleven disciples went to Galilee, to the mountain to which Jesus had directed them. When they saw him, they worshiped him; but some doubted. And Jesus came and said to them, "All authority in heaven and on earth has been given to me. Go therefore and make disciples of all nations, baptizing them in the name of the Father and of the Son and of the Holy Spirit, and teaching them to obey everything that I have commanded you. And remember, I am with you always, to the end of the age."

Matt. 3:16–17 And when Jesus had been baptized, just as he came up from the water, suddenly the heavens were opened to him and he saw the Spirit of God descending like a dove and alighting on him. And a voice from heaven said, "This is my Son, the Beloved, with whom I am well pleased."

1 Peter 1:2 [To those] who have been chosen and destined by God the Father and sanctified by the Spirit to be obedient to Jesus Christ and to be sprinkled with his blood: May grace and peace be yours in abundance.

1 Cor. 12:4–6 Now there are varieties of gifts, but the same Spirit; and there are varieties of services, but the same Lord; and there are varieties of activities, but it is the same God who activates all of them in everyone.

Question 59. What is the meaning of this name?

It is the name of the Holy Trinity. The Father is God, the Son is God, and the Holy Spirit is God. And yet they are not three gods, but one God in three persons. We worship God in this mystery.

2 Cor. 13:13 The grace of the Lord Jesus Christ, the love of God, and the communion of the Holy Spirit be with all of you.

John 1:1–4 In the beginning was the Word, and the Word was with God, and the Word was God. He was in the beginning with God. All things came into being through him, and without him not one thing came into being. What has come into being in him was life, and the life was the light of all people.

Rom. 8:11 If the Spirit of him who raised Jesus from the dead dwells in you, he who raised Christ from the dead will give life to your mortal bodies also through his Spirit that dwells in you.

John 16:13–15 When the Spirit of truth comes, he will guide you into all the truth; for he will not speak on his own, but will speak whatever he hears, and he will declare to you the things that are to come. He will glorify me, because he will take what is mine and declare it to you. All that the Father has is mine. For this reason I said that he will take what is mine and declare it to you.

Question 60. What is the Lord's Supper?

The Lord's Supper is the sign and seal by which our communion with Christ is renewed.

1 Cor. 10:16 The cup of blessing that we bless, is it not a sharing in the blood of Christ? The bread that we break, is it not a sharing in the body of Christ?

Question 61. What does it mean to share in the Lord's Supper?

When we celebrate the Lord's Supper, the Lord Jesus Christ is truly present, pouring out his Spirit upon us. By his Spirit, the bread that we break and the cup that we bless share in his body and blood. As I receive the bread and the cup, remembering that Christ died even for me, I feed on him in my heart by faith with thanksgiving. His life becomes mine, and my life becomes his, to all eternity.

1 Cor. 11:23–26 For I received from the Lord what I also handed on to you, that the Lord Jesus on the night when he was betrayed took a loaf of bread, and when he had given thanks, he broke it and said, "This is my body that is for you. Do this in remembrance of me." In the same way he took the cup also, after supper, saying, "This cup is the new covenant in my blood. Do this, as often as you drink it, in remembrance of me." For as often as you eat this bread and drink the cup, you proclaim the Lord's death until he comes.

Mark 14:22–25 While they were eating, he took a loaf of bread, and after blessing it he broke it, gave it to them, and said, "Take; this is my body." Then he took a cup, and after giving thanks he gave it to them, and all of them drank from it. He said to them, "This is my blood of the covenant, which is poured out for many. Truly I tell you, I will never again drink of the fruit of the vine until that day when I drink it new in the kingdom of God."

Question 62. What do you mean when you speak of "the forgiveness of sins"?

Because of Jesus Christ, God no longer holds my sins against me. Christ alone is my righteousness and my life. Grace alone is the basis on which God has forgiven me in him. Faith alone is the means by which I receive Christ into my heart, and with him the forgiveness that makes me whole.

1 Cor. 1:30 He is the source of your life in Christ Jesus, who became for us wisdom from God, and righteousness and sanctification and redemption. . . .

1 Tim. 1:1 Paul, an apostle of Christ Jesus by the command of God our Savior and of Christ Jesus our hope. . .

Rom. 11:6 But if it is by grace, it is no longer on the basis of works, otherwise grace would no longer be grace.

Eph. 2:8 For by grace you have been saved through faith, and this is not your own doing; it is the gift of God. . . .

Rom. 5:15 But the free gift is not like the trespass. For if the many died through the one man's trespass, much more surely have the grace of God and the free gift in the grace of the one man, Jesus Christ, abounded for the many.

Rom. 4:16 For this reason it depends on faith, in order that the promise may rest on grace and be guaranteed to all his descendants, not only to the adherents of the law but also to those who share the faith of Abraham (for he is the father of all of us). . . .

Rom. 3:28 For we hold that a person is justified by faith apart from works prescribed by the law.

Question 63. Does forgiveness mean that God excuses sin?

No. God does not cease to be God. Although God is merciful to the sinner, God does not excuse the evil of sin. For to forgive is not to excuse.

Hab. 1:13 Your eyes are too pure to behold evil, and you cannot look on wrongdoing; why do you look on the treacherous, and are silent when the wicked swallow those more righteous than they?

Isa. 59:15 Truth is lacking, and whoever turns from evil is despoiled. The LORD saw it, and it displeased him that there was no justice.

Heb. 9:22 Indeed, under the law almost everything is purified with blood, and without the shedding of blood there is no forgiveness of sins.

Rom. 5:8–10 But God proves his love for us in that while we still were sinners Christ died for us. Much more surely then, now that we have been justified by his blood, will we be saved through him from the wrath of God. For if while we were enemies, we were reconciled to God through the death of his Son, much more surely, having been reconciled, will we be saved by his life.

1 Chron. 16:33 Then shall the trees of the forest sing for joy before the LORD, for he comes to judge the earth.

Question 64. Does your forgiveness of those who have harmed you depend on their repentance?

No. I am to forgive as I have been forgiven. Just as God's forgiveness of me does not depend on my first confessing and repenting of my sins, so my forgiveness of those who harm me does not depend on their doing so. However, when I forgive the person who has harmed me, I do not deny or excuse the harm that was done.

Col. 3:13 Bear with one another and, if anyone has a complaint against another, forgive each other; just as the Lord has forgiven you, so you also must forgive.

Mark 11:25 Whenever you stand praying, forgive, if you have anything against anyone; so that your Father in heaven may also forgive you your trespasses.

Col. 2:13 And when you were dead in trespasses and the uncircumcision of your flesh, God made you alive together with him, when he forgave us all our trespasses. . . .

Matt. 18:21–22 Then Peter came and said to him, "Lord, if another member of the church sins against me, how often should I forgive? As many as seven times?" Jesus said to him, "Not seven times, but, I tell you, seventy-seven times."

Heb. 12:14 Pursue peace with everyone, and the holiness without which no one will see the Lord.

Question 65. What do you mean when you speak of "the resurrection of the body"?

Because Christ lives, we will live also. Death is not the end of human life. The whole person, body and soul, will be raised from death to eternal life with God.

John 14:19 In a little while the world will no longer see me, but you will see me; because I live, you also will live.

John 11:25 Jesus said to her, "I am the resurrection and the life. Those who believe in me, even though they die, will live. . . ."

Rom. 6:5 For if we have been united with him in a death like his, we will certainly be united with him in a resurrection like his.

1 Cor. 15:21 For since death came through a human being, the resurrection of the dead has also come through a human being. . . .

1 Cor. 15:42 So it is with the resurrection of the dead. What is sown is perishable, what is raised is imperishable.

Col. 1:18 He is the head of the body, the church; he is the beginning, the firstborn from the dead, so that he might come to have first place in everything.

Question 66. What do you affirm when you speak of "the life everlasting"?

God does not will to be God without us, but instead grants to us creatures—fallen and mortal as we are—eternal life. Communion with Jesus Christ is eternal life itself.

John 3:16 For God so loved the world that he gave his only Son, so that everyone who believes in him may not perish but may have eternal life.

John 6:54 Those who eat my flesh and drink my blood have eternal life, and I will raise them up on the last day. . . .

John 17:3 And this is eternal life, that they may know you, the only true God, and Jesus Christ whom you have sent.

Rom. 6:22 But now that you have been freed from sin and enslaved to God, the advantage you get is sanctification. The end is eternal life.

Rom. 6:23 For the wages of sin is death, but the free gift of God is eternal life in Christ Jesus our Lord.

1 John 2:25 And this is what he has promised us, eternal life.

Matt. 25:34 Then the king will say to those at his right hand, "Come, you that are blessed by my Father, inherit the kingdom prepared for you from the foundation of the world. . . ."

Question 67. Won't heaven be a boring place?

No. Heaven is our true home, a world of love. There we shall at last see face to face what we now only glimpse as through a distant mirror. Our deepest, truest delights in this life are only a dim foreshadowing of the delights that await us in heaven.

John 14:2–3 In my Father's house there are many dwelling places. If it were not so, would I have told you that I go to prepare a place for you? And if I go and prepare a place for you, I will come again and will take you to myself, so that where I am, there you may be also.

Matt. 6:20 But store up for yourselves treasures in heaven, where neither moth nor rust consumes and where thieves do not break in and steal.

Matt. 8:11 I tell you, many will come from east and west and will eat with Abraham and Isaac and Jacob in the kingdom of heaven. . . .

Col. 1:5 . . . because of the hope laid up for you in heaven. You have heard of this hope before in the word of the truth, the gospel. . . .

1 Cor. 13:12 For now we see in a mirror, dimly, but then we will see face to face. Now I know only in part; then I will know fully, even as I have been fully known.

II. The Ten Commandments

Question 68. What are the Ten Commandments?

The Ten Commandments give a summary of God's law for our lives. They teach us how to live rightly with God and one another.

Deut. 10:4 Then he wrote on the tablets the same words as before, the ten commandments that the LORD had spoken to you on the mountain out of the fire on the day of the assembly; and the LORD gave them to me.

Matt. 19:17 And he said to him, "Why do you ask me about what is good? There is only one who is good. If you wish to enter into life, keep the commandments."

Question 69. Why should you obey this law?

Not to win God's love, for God already loves me. Not to earn my salvation, for Christ has earned it for me. Not to avoid being punished, for then I would obey out of fear. With gladness in my heart I should obey God's law out of gratitude, for God has blessed me by it and given it for my well-being.

Ps. 118:1 O give thanks to the LORD, for he is good; his steadfast love endures forever!

Col. 3:17 And whatever you do, in word or deed, do everything in the name of the Lord Jesus, giving thanks to God the Father through him.

Question 70. What is the first commandment?

You shall have no other gods before me (Ex. 20:3; Deut. 5:7).

Deut. 26:17 Today you have obtained the LORD's agreement: to be your God; and for you to walk in his ways, to keep his statutes, his commandments, and his ordinances, and to obey him.

Matt. 4:10 Jesus said to him, "Away with you, Satan! for it is written, 'Worship the Lord your God, and serve only him.'"

Question 71. What do you learn from this commandment?

No loyalty comes before my loyalty to God. I should worship and serve only God, expect all good from God alone, and love, fear, and honor God with all my heart.

Matt. 6:24 No one can serve two masters; for a slave will either hate the one and love the other, or be devoted to the one and despise the other. You cannot serve God and wealth.

Deut. 6:5 You shall love the LORD your God with all your heart, and with all your soul, and with all your might.

Prov. 9:10 The fear of the LORD is the beginning of wisdom, and the knowledge of the Holy One is insight.

Matt. 10:37 Whoever loves father or mother more than me is not worthy of me; and whoever loves son or daughter more than me is not worthy of me. . . .

Question 72. What is the second commandment?

You shall not make for yourself an idol (Ex. 20:4; Deut. 5:8).

Question 73. What do you learn from this commandment?

First, when I treat anything other than God as though it were God, I make it an idol. Second, when I assume that my own interests are more important than anything else, I make them into idols, and in effect I also make an idol of myself.

Deut. 6:14 Do not follow other gods, any of the gods of the peoples who are all around you. . . .

1 John 5:21 Little children, keep yourselves from idols.

Ex. 34:14 For you shall worship no other god, because the LORD, whose name is Jealous, is a jealous God.

1 Chron. 16:26 For all the gods of the peoples are idols, but the LORD made the heavens.

Rom. 1:22–23 Claiming to be wise, they became fools; and they exchanged the glory of the immortal God for images resembling a mortal human being or birds or four-footed animals or reptiles.

Phil. 2:4   Let each of you look not to your own interests, but to the interests of others.

Question 74. What is the third commandment?

You shall not make wrongful use of the name of the Lord your God (Ex. 20:7; Deut. 5:11).

Question 75. What do you learn from this commandment?

I should use God's name with reverence and awe. God's name is holy and deserves the highest honor from us. It is insulted when used carelessly, as in a curse or a pious cliché.

Ps. 29:2   Ascribe to the LORD the glory of his name; worship the LORD in holy splendor.

Rev. 15:3–4   And they sing the song of Moses, the servant of God, and the song of the Lamb: "Great and amazing are your deeds, Lord God the Almighty! Just and true are your ways, King of the nations! Lord, who will not fear and glorify your name? For you alone are holy. All nations will come and worship before you, for your judgments have been revealed."

Ps. 138:2   I bow down toward your holy temple and give thanks to your name for your steadfast love and your faithfulness; for you have exalted your name and your word above everything.

Eph. 4:29   Let no evil talk come out of your mouths, but only what is useful for building up, as there is need, so that your words may give grace to those who hear.

Ps. 103:1–2   Bless the LORD, O my soul, and all that is within me, bless his holy name. Bless the LORD, O my soul, and do not forget all his benefits. . . .

Question 76. What is the fourth commandment?

Remember the Sabbath day, and keep it holy (Ex. 20:8; Deut. 5:12).

Question 77. What do you learn from this commandment?

God requires a special day to be set apart so that worship can be at the center of my life. It is right to honor God with thanks and praise, and to hear and receive God's Word.

> *Rom. 10:8* But what does it say? "The word is near you, on your lips and in your heart" (that is, the word of faith that we proclaim). . . .

> *Deut. 5:12* Observe the sabbath day and keep it holy, as the LORD your God commanded you.

> *Gen. 2:3* So God blessed the seventh day and hallowed it, because on it God rested from all the work that he had done in creation.

> *Lev. 23:3* Six days shall work be done; but the seventh day is a sabbath of complete rest, a holy convocation; you shall do no work: it is a sabbath to the LORD throughout your settlements.

> *Acts 2:42,46* They devoted themselves to the apostles' teaching and fellowship, to the breaking of bread and the prayers. . . . Day by day, as they spent much time together in the temple, they broke bread at home and ate their food with glad and generous hearts. . . .

Question 78. What is the best summary of the first four commandments?

These teach me how to live rightly with God. Jesus summed them up with the commandment he called the first and greatest: You shall love the Lord your God with all your heart, and with all your soul, and with all your mind (Matt. 22:37; Deut. 6:5).

Question 79. What is the fifth commandment?

Honor your father and your mother (Ex. 20:12; Deut. 5:16).

Question 80. What do you learn from this commandment?

Though I owe reverence to God alone, I owe genuine respect to my parents, both my mother and father. God wills me to listen to them, be thankful for the benefits I receive from them, and be considerate of their needs, especially in old age.

Eph. 5:21 Be subject to one another out of reverence for Christ.

Rom. 12:10 Love one another with mutual affection; outdo one another in showing honor.

Eph. 6:2 "Honor your father and mother"—this is the first commandment with a promise. . . .

Prov. 1:8 Hear, my child, your father's instruction, and do not reject your mother's teaching. . . .

Lev. 19:32 You shall rise before the aged, and defer to the old; and you shall fear your God: I am the LORD.

Luke 2:51 Then he went down with them and came to Nazareth, and was obedient to them. His mother treasured all these things in her heart.

Question 81. Are there limits to your obligation to obey them?

Yes. No mere human being is God. Blind obedience is not required, for everything should be tested by loyalty and obedience to God.

1 Peter 2:17 Honor everyone. Love the family of believers. Fear God. Honor the emperor.

Acts 5:29 Peter and the apostles answered, "We must obey God rather than any human authority."

Question 82. What is the sixth commandment?

You shall not murder (Ex. 20:13; Deut. 5:17).

Question 83. What do you learn from this commandment?

God forbids anything that harms my neighbor unfairly. Murder or injury can be done not only by direct violence but also by an angry word or a clever plan, and not only by an individual but also by unjust social institutions. I should honor every human being, including my enemy, as a person made in God's image.

1 John 3:15 All who hate a brother or sister are murderers, and you know that murderers do not have eternal life abiding in them.

Prov. 24:17 Do not rejoice when your enemies fall, and do not let your heart be glad when they stumble. . . .

Rom. 12:19–20 Beloved, never avenge yourselves, but leave room for the wrath of God; for it is written, "Vengeance is mine, I will repay, says the Lord." No, "if your enemies are hungry, feed them; if they are thirsty, give them something to drink; for by doing this you will heap burning coals on their heads."

Col. 3:12–13 "As God's chosen ones, holy and beloved, clothe yourselves with compassion, kindness, humility, meekness, and patience. Bear with one another and, if anyone has a complaint against another, forgive each other; just as the Lord has forgiven you, so you also must forgive.

Matt. 5:21–22 You have heard that it was said to those of ancient times, "You shall not murder"; and "whoever murders shall be liable to judgment." But I say to you that if you are angry with a brother or sister, you will be liable to judgment; and if you insult a brother or sister, you will be liable to the council; and if you say, "You fool," you will be liable to the hell of fire.

Matt. 26:52 Then Jesus said to him, "Put your sword back into its place; for all who take the sword will perish by the sword."

Question 84. What is the seventh commandment?

You shall not commit adultery (Ex. 20:14; Deut. 5:18).

Question 85. What do you learn from this commandment?

God requires fidelity and purity in sexual relations. Since love is God's great gift, God expects me not to corrupt it, or confuse it with momentary desire or the selfish fulfillment of my own pleasures. God forbids all sexual immorality, whether in married or in single life.

> *Eph. 5:3* But fornication and impurity of any kind, or greed, must not even be mentioned among you, as is proper among saints.

> *Matt. 5:27–29* You have heard that it was said, "You shall not commit adultery." But I say to you that everyone who looks at a woman with lust has already committed adultery with her in his heart. If your right eye causes you to sin, tear it out and throw it away; it is better for you to lose one of your members than for your whole body to be thrown into hell.

> *Heb. 13:4* Let marriage be held in honor by all, and let the marriage bed be kept undefiled; for God will judge fornicators and adulterers.

> *1 Thess. 4:3–4* For this is the will of God, your sanctification: that you abstain from fornication; that each one of you know how to control your own body in holiness and honor. . . .

Question 86. What is the eighth commandment?

You shall not steal (Ex. 20:15; Deut. 5:19).

Question 87. What do you learn from this commandment?

God forbids all theft and robbery, including schemes, tricks, or systems that unjustly take what belongs to someone else.

God requires me not to be driven by greed, not to misuse or waste the gifts I have been given, and not to distrust the promise that God will supply my needs.

Job 20:19–20 For they have crushed and abandoned the poor, they have seized a house that they did not build. "They knew no quiet in their bellies; in their greed they let nothing escape."

Jer. 22:13 Woe to him who builds his house by unrighteousness, and his upper rooms by injustice; who makes his neighbors work for nothing, and does not give them their wages. . . .

Prov. 18.9 One who is slack in work is close kin to a vandal.

1 Tim. 6:9–10 But those who want to be rich fall into temptation and are trapped by many senseless and harmful desires that plunge people into ruin and destruction. For the love of money is the root of all kinds of evil, and in their eagerness to be rich some have wandered away from the faith and pierced themselves with many pains.

1 John 3:17 How does God's love abide in anyone who has the world's goods and sees a brother or sister in need and yet refuses help?

Luke 12:15 And he said to them, "Take care! Be on your guard against all kinds of greed; for one's life does not consist in the abundance of possessions."

Phil. 4:19 And my God will fully satisfy every need of yours according to his riches in glory in Christ Jesus.

Question 88. What is the ninth commandment?

You shall not bear false witness against your neighbor (Ex. 20:16; Deut. 5:20).

Question 89. What do you learn from this commandment?

God forbids me to damage the honor or reputation of my neighbor. I should not say false things against anyone for the sake of money, favor, or friendship, for the sake of revenge, or for any other reason. God requires me to speak well of my neighbor when I can, and to view the faults of my neighbor with tolerance when I cannot.

> *Zech. 8:16–17* These are the things that you shall do: Speak the truth to one another, render in your gates judgments that are true and make for peace, do not devise evil in your hearts against one another, and love no false oath; for all these are things that I hate, says the LORD.

> *1 Peter 3:16* Keep your conscience clear, so that, when you are maligned, those who abuse you for your good conduct in Christ may be put to shame.

> *Prov. 14:5* A faithful witness does not lie, but a false witness breathes out lies.

> *James 4:11* Do not speak evil against one another, brothers and sisters. Whoever speaks evil against another or judges another, speaks evil against the law and judges the law; but if you judge the law, you are not a doer of the law but a judge.

> *1 Peter 4:8* Above all, maintain constant love for one another, for love covers a multitude of sins.

Question 90. Does this commandment forbid racism and other forms of negative stereotyping?

Yes. In forbidding false witness against my neighbor, God forbids me to be prejudiced against people who belong to any vulnerable, different, or disfavored social group. Jews, women, homosexuals, racial and ethnic minorities, and national enemies are among those who have suffered terribly from being subjected to the slurs of social prejudice.

> *Rom. 3:13, 15* "Their throats are opened graves; they use their tongues to deceive." "The venom of vipers is under their lips." . . . "Their feet are swift to shed blood."

> *Prov. 31:8–9* Speak out for those who cannot speak, for the rights of all the destitute. Speak out, judge righteously, defend the rights of the poor and needy.

> *Matt. 7:1–2* Do not judge, so that you may not be judged. For with the judgment you make you will be judged, and the measure you give will be the measure you get.

Question 91. What is the tenth commandment?

You shall not covet what is your neighbor's (Ex. 20:17; Deut. 5:21).

Question 92. What do you learn from this commandment?

My whole heart should belong to God alone, not to money or the things of this world. "Coveting" means desiring something wrongfully. I should not resent the good fortune or success of my neighbor or allow envy to corrupt my heart.

> *Heb. 13:5* Keep your lives free from the love of money, and be content with what you have; for he has said, "I will never leave you or forsake you."

> *Gal. 5:26* Let us not become conceited, competing against one another, envying one another.

Question 93. What is the best summary of the last six commandments?

> These teach me how to live rightly with my neighbor. Jesus summed them up with a commandment which is

like the greatest one about loving God: You shall love your neighbor as yourself (Matt. 22:39; Lev. 19:18).

Question 94. Can you obey these commandments perfectly?

No. Yet there is more grace in God than sin in me. While I must confess my sins to God and resolve not to commit them, I can be confident that God is forgiving, and will give me the grace to grow in love and knowledge day by day.

Ps. 14:3 They have all gone astray, they are all alike perverse; there is no one who does good, no, not one.

Eph. 2:8 For by grace you have been saved through faith, and this is not your own doing; it is the gift of God. . .

Ps. 130:3–4 If you, O LORD, should mark iniquities, Lord, who could stand? But there is forgiveness with you, so that you may be revered.

Col. 1:13–14 He has rescued us from the power of darkness and transferred us into the kingdom of his beloved Son, in whom we have redemption, the forgiveness of sins.

1 John 1:8 If we say that we have no sin, we deceive ourselves, and the truth is not in us.

III. The Lord's Prayer

Question 95. What is prayer?

Prayer means calling upon God whose Spirit is always present with us. In prayer we approach God with reverence, confidence, and humility. Prayer involves both addressing God in praise, confession, thanksgiving, and supplication, and listening for God's word within our hearts. When we adore God, we are filled with wonder, love, and praise before God's heavenly glory. When we confess our sins to God, we ask for forgiveness with sorry hearts. When we give thanks to God, we acknowledge God's great goodness in all that has been provided for us. Finally, when we call upon God to hear our requests, we affirm that God is always near to us in times of need and sorrow.

Ps. 48:1 Great is the LORD and greatly to be praised in the city of our God.

Ps. 96:8–9 Ascribe to the LORD the glory due his name; bring an offering, and come into his courts. Worship the LORD in holy splendor; tremble before him, all the earth.

James 5:16 Therefore confess your sins to one another, and pray for one another, so that you may be healed. The prayer of the righteous is powerful and effective.

1 John 1:9 If we confess our sins, he who is faithful and just will forgive us our sins and cleanse us from all unrighteousness.

Ps. 107:8 Let them thank the LORD for his steadfast love, for his wonderful works to humankind.

Ps. 75:1 We give thanks to you, O God; we give thanks; your name is near. People tell of your wondrous deeds.

Ps. 50:15 Call on me in the day of trouble; I will deliver you, and you shall glorify me.

Ps. 145:18 The LORD is near to all who call on him, to all who call on him in truth.

Eph. 6:18 Pray in the Spirit at all times in every prayer and supplication. To that end keep alert and always persevere in supplication for all the saints.

Question 96. What is the purpose of prayer?

Prayer brings us into communion with God. The more our lives are rooted in prayer, the more we sense how wonderful God is in grace, purity, majesty, and love.

Prayer means offering our lives completely to God, submitting ourselves to God's will, and waiting faithfully for God's grace. Through prayer God frees us from anxiety, equips us for service, and deepens our faith.

Ps. 62:8 Trust in him at all times, O people; pour out your heart before him; God is a refuge for us.

Ps. 139:1 O LORD, you have searched me and known me.

Phil. 4:6 Do not worry about anything, but in everything by prayer and supplication with thanksgiving let your requests be made known to God.

Matt. 7:7–8 Ask, and it will be given you; search, and you will find; knock, and the door will be opened for you. For everyone who asks receives, and everyone who searches finds, and for everyone who knocks, the door will be opened.

Question 97. What prayer serves as our rule or pattern?

Our rule or pattern is found in the Lord's Prayer, which Jesus taught to his disciples:

> Our Father in heaven,
>> hallowed be your name,
>> your kingdom come,
>> your will be done,
>>> on earth as in heaven.
>
> Give us today our daily bread.
> Forgive us our sins
>> as we forgive those who sin against us.
>
> Save us from the time of trial
>> and deliver us from evil.
>
> For the kingdom, the power, and the glory
>> are yours now and for ever. Amen.

These words express everything that we may desire and expect from God.

Question 98. What is meant by addressing God as "Our Father in heaven"?

When we pray to God as "our Father in heaven," we draw near with childlike reverence and place ourselves securely in God's hands. We express our confidence that God cares for us, and that nothing on earth is beyond the reach of God's grace.

> *Rom. 8:15–16* For you did not receive a spirit of slavery to fall back into fear, but you have received a spirit of adoption. When we cry, "Abba! Father!" it is that very Spirit bearing witness with our spirit that we are children of God. . . .

> *Jer. 23:23–24* Am I a God near by, says the LORD, and not a God far off? Who can hide in secret places so that I cannot see them? says the LORD. Do I not fill heaven and earth? says the LORD.

> *Acts 17:24–25* The God who made the world and everything in it, he who is Lord of heaven and earth, does not live in shrines made by human hands, nor is he served by human hands, as though he needed anything, since he himself gives to all mortals life and breath and all things.

Question 99. What is meant by the first petition, "Hallowed be your name"?

This petition is placed first, because it expresses the goal and purpose of the whole prayer. When we pray for God's name to be "hallowed," we ask that we will know and glorify God as God really is, and that all things will truly come to serve God.

> *Jer. 9:23–24* Thus says the LORD: Do not let the wise boast in their wisdom, do not let the mighty boast in their might, do not let the wealthy boast in their wealth; but let those who boast boast in this, that they understand and

know me, that I am the LORD; I act with steadfast love, justice, and righteousness in the earth, for in these things I delight, says the LORD.

Rom. 11:36 For from him and through him and to him are all things. To him be the glory forever. Amen.

Ps. 115:1 Not to us, O LORD, not to us, but to your name give glory, for the sake of your steadfast love and your faithfulness.

Question 100. What is meant by the second petition, "Your kingdom come"?

We ask God to come and rule among us through faith, love, and justice. We pray for both the church and the world, that God will rule in our hearts through faith, in our personal relationships through love, and in our institutional affairs through justice.

Ps. 68:1 Let God rise up, let his enemies be scattered; let those who hate him flee before him.

2 Thess. 3:1 Finally, brothers and sisters, pray for us, so that the word of the Lord may spread rapidly and be glorified everywhere, just as it is among you. . . .

Rev. 22:20 The one who testifies to these things says, "Surely I am coming soon." Amen. Come, Lord Jesus!

Rom. 8:22–24 We know that the whole creation has been groaning in labor pains until now; and not only the creation, but we ourselves, who have the first fruits of the Spirit, groan inwardly while we wait for adoption, the redemption of our bodies. For in hope we were saved. Now hope that is seen is not hope. For who hopes for what is seen?

1 Cor. 15:20, 28 But in fact Christ has been raised from the dead, the first fruits of those who have died. . . . When all things are subjected to him, then the Son himself will also be subjected to the one who put all things in subjection under him, so that God may be all in all.

Question 101. What is meant by the third petition, "Your will be done, on earth as in heaven"?

Of course, God's will is always done and will surely come to pass, whether we desire it or not. But the phrase "on earth as in heaven" means that we ask for the grace to do God's will on earth in the way that it is done in heaven—gladly and from the heart. We yield ourselves, in life and in death, to God's will.

> *Ps. 119:34–36* Give me understanding, that I may keep your law and observe it with my whole heart. Lead me in the path of your commandments, for I delight in it. Turn my heart to your decrees, and not to selfish gain.

> *Ps. 103:20, 22* Bless the LORD, O you his angels, you mighty ones who do his bidding, obedient to his spoken word. . . . Bless the LORD, all his works, in all places of his dominion. Bless the LORD, O my soul.

> *Luke 22:42* Father, if you are willing, remove this cup from me; yet, not my will but yours be done.

> *Rom. 12:2* Do not be conformed to this world, but be transformed by the renewing of your minds, so that you may discern what is the will of God—what is good and acceptable and perfect.

Question 102. What is meant by the fourth petition, "Give us today our daily bread"?

We ask God to supply all our needs, for we know that God, who cares for us in every area of our life, has promised to give us temporal as well as spiritual blessings. God commands us to pray each day for all that we need and no more, so that we will learn to rely completely on God.

Prov. 30:8 Remove far from me falsehood and lying; give me neither poverty nor riches; feed me with the food that I need. . . .

Ps. 90:17 Let the favor of the Lord our God be upon us, and prosper for us the work of our hands—O prosper the work of our hands!

Ps. 55:22 Cast your burden on the LORD, and he will sustain you; he will never permit the righteous to be moved.

Ps. 72:4 May he defend the cause of the poor of the people, give deliverance to the needy, and crush the oppressor.

Ps. 104:27–28 These all look to you to give them their food in due season; when you give to them, they gather it up; when you open your hand, they are filled with good things.

Question 103. What is meant by the fifth petition, "Forgive us our sins as we forgive those who sin against us"?

We pray that a new and right spirit will be put within us. We ask for the grace to treat others with the same mercy we have received from God. We ask that we will not resent or strike back at those who harm us, but that our hearts will be knit together with the merciful heart of God.

Matt. 18:33 Should you not have had mercy on your fellow slave, as I had mercy on you?

Matt. 6:14–15 For if you forgive others their trespasses, your heavenly Father will also forgive you; but if you do not forgive others, neither will your Father forgive your trespasses.

Ps. 51:10 Create in me a clean heart, O God, and put a new and right spirit within me.

1 John 2:1–2 My little children, I am writing these things to you so that you may not sin. But if anyone does sin, we have an advocate with the Father, Jesus Christ the righteous; and he is the atoning sacrifice for our sins, and not for ours only but also for the sins of the whole world.

Question 104. What is meant by the final petition, "Save us from the time of trial and deliver us from evil"?

We ask God to protect us from all that threatens to hurt or destroy us. We pray for the ability to resist sin and evil in our own lives, and for the grace to endure suffering in trust and without bitterness when it is unavoidable. We ask for the grace to believe in the love of God that will finally swallow up all the evil and hatred in the world.

2 Cor. 4:8 We are afflicted in every way, but not crushed; perplexed, but not driven to despair. . . .

Eph. 3:19 . . . and to know the love of Christ that surpasses knowledge, so that you may be filled with all the fullness of God.

Matt. 26:41 Stay awake and pray that you may not come into the time of trial; the spirit indeed is willing, but the flesh is weak.

Question 105. What is meant by the closing doxology, "For the kingdom, the power, and the glory are yours now and for ever"?

We give God thanks and praise for the kingdom more powerful than all enemies, for the power perfected in the weakness of love, and for the glory that includes our well-being and that of the whole creation, both now and to all eternity.

Rev. 5:12 Worthy is the Lamb that was slaughtered to receive power and wealth and wisdom and might and honor and glory and blessing!

Rev. 4:11 You are worthy, our Lord and God, to receive glory and honor and power, for you created all things, and by your will they existed and were created.

1 Chron. 29:11, 13 Yours, O LORD, are the greatness, the power, the glory, the victory, and the majesty; for all that is in the heavens and on the earth is yours; yours is the kingdom, O LORD, and you are exalted as head above all. . . . And now, our God, we give thanks to you and praise your glorious name.

Question 106. What is meant by the word "Amen"?

"Amen" means "so be it" or "let it be so." It expresses our complete confidence in the triune God, the God of the covenant with Israel as fulfilled through our Lord Jesus Christ, who makes no promise that will not be kept, and whose mercy endures forever.

Rev. 22:20 The one who testifies to these things says, "Surely I am coming soon." Amen. Come, Lord Jesus!

2 Cor. 1:20 For in him every one of God's promises is a "Yes." For this reason it is through him that we say the "Amen," to the glory of God.

2 Tim. 2:13 If we are faithless, he remains faithful—for he cannot deny himself.